Learn letter blends with Blip

A **br**idge for my **br**other

Learn letter bl... Blip

First published in the UK in 2006 by QED Publishing
A Quarto Group company
226 City Road
London EC1V 2TT
www.qed-publishing.co.uk

Reprinted in 2007

A Catalogue record for this book is available from the British Library.

ISBN 978 1 84538 859 1

Written by Wendy Body
Designed by Alix Wood
Editor Gina Nuttall
Illustrations Caroline Martin

Publisher Steve Evans
Editorial Director Jean Coppendale
Art Director Zeta Davies

Printed and bound in China

A **cr**own for the **cr**ocodile

A **dr**um and a **dr**agon

Fruit for my frog

Grapes for **gr**anddad

A **pr**esent for the **pr**incess

A **tr**ain and a **tr**umpet

A **bl**anket and some **bl**ueberries

A **cl**oak for the **cl**own

A **fl**ag and some **fl**owers

Some **gl**oves and some **gl**itter

Plenty of plums and plants

A **sl**eigh and a **sl**ide

A scarf for school

A **sk**ateboard for the **sk**eleton

Some **sn**owdrops and a **sn**ake

Spoons for the **sp**ider

Stamps and a **st**arfish

A **sw**ing for the **sw**an...

And a small truck to bring it all home!

Parents' and teachers' notes

• Before reading the book, read the title and look at the front cover illustration with your child. Talk about what the character is (a monster), what his name is (Blip) and what Blip is doing. Can your child think of any words that rhyme with Blip?

• As you read the book to your child, run your finger along underneath the text. This will help your child to follow the reading and focus on how the words both look and sound.

• On the first or second rereading, leave out some of the words being used to illustrate the letter sounds and let your child say them. Point to the illustration to help your child supply the word.

• Draw your child's attention to the beginning of words – e.g. "This word begins with an **n** (letter name) and it makes a **nnnnnn** sound." or "This word begins with **s** (letter name) and an **h**. When we put them together they make a **shhh** sound."

• When you are talking about letter sounds, try not to add too much of an **uh** or **er** sound. Say **mmm** instead of **muh** or **mer**, **ssss** instead of **suh** or **ser**. Saying letter sounds as carefully as possible helps children when they are trying to build up or spell words: **fer-o-rer** doesn't sound much like **for**!

• Talk about and discuss the characters on each page – what they look like, what they are doing and why, and what they might be thinking.

• Encourage your child to express opinions and preferences – e.g. "Which picture do you like most?" "Which part of the book did you like best? Why?"

• Choose any page and use the illustration to play "I Spy" using letter sounds rather than names.

• Make a set of cards, each with one of the initial consonant blends covered in the book. Give your child a card and ask him or her to match the card to words in the book that begin with that letter blend.

• Make a shopping list with your child. Can your child think of an item for each of the initial letter blends in the book?

• Collect objects beginning with some of the letter blends in the book (e.g. brick, glove, flower, plum, grape). Say words with those blends (but not the object names). Ask your child to pick up the object that begins with the same sound.

• Talk about words: their meaning, how they sound, how they look and how they are spelled. However, if your child gets restless or bored, stop. Enjoyment of the book or activity is essential if we want children to grow up valuing books and reading!